DEBRA OSWALD is a writer for stage, television and children's fiction.

Debra's stage plays have been produced around Australia. *Gary's House*, *Sweet Road* and *The Peach Season* were all shortlisted for the NSW Premier's Literary Award and her play *Dags* has had many Australian productions. *Gary's House* has been performed in translation in Denmark and Japan. *Mr Bailey's Minder* broke the Griffin Theatre's box office record in 2004, toured nationally in 2006 and was produced in Philadelphia in 2008.

Debra has written three plays for the Australian Theatre for Young People – *Skate*, *Stories in the Dark* (NSW Premier's Literary Play Award in 2008) and *House on Fire* (2010). Eight of Debra's plays are published by Currency Press.

She's the co-creator and head writer of the award-winning Channel Ten series *Offspring*. The fifth series of *Offspring* goes to air in 2014. Debra won the 2011 NSW Premier's Literary Award for the Offspring telemovie script and won the 2014 AACTA for Best Television Screenplay for an episode in series 4. Her other television credits include award-winning episodes of *Police Rescue*, *Palace of Dreams*, *The Secret Life Of Us*, *Sweet and Sour* and *Bananas in Pyjamas*.

She is the author of three 'Aussie Bite' books for kids, including *Nathan and the Ice Rockets*, and six novels for teenage readers including *The Redback Leftovers* and *Blue Noise*. Her first novel for adults, *Useful*, will be published by Penguin in 2014/15.

Also by Debra Oswald

DAGS

Debra Oswald

Currency Press • Sydney

First published in 1987
by Currency Press Pty Ltd
PO Box 2287, Strawberry Hills, NSW, 2012, Australia
enquiries@currency.com.au; www.currency.com.au

Copyright © Debra Oswald 1987

Reprinted 1989, 1990, 1992, 1993, 1994, 1997, 1999, 2002, 2003, 2004, 2006, 2008, 2011, 2014, 2016, 2018

Cataloguing-in-publication data for this title is available from the National Library of Australia website.
Cover design by Jana Hartig
Printed by Ligare Book Printers, Riverwood

for Richard Glover

Dags was commissioned by the Canberra Youth Theatre and was first performed at the Seymour Centre, Sydney on 9 May, 1985, with the following cast:

GILLIAN	Megan Cameron
WENDY/KAREN	Diana Carr
ADAM/TONY/BIGGLES/	
DEREK	Ben Grieve
BRONWYN	Ursla Hawthorne
LYNETTE/MONICA	Mary Stansfield

Directed by Gail Kelly
Designed by Fred Lynn

All photographs in this book are from the Toe Truck production, first performed at the Seymour Centre in Sydney on 19 July 1986. Photographer: Sandy Edwards.

Thank you/thank you/thank you…

The author would like to thank Penny Bond, the Literature Board of the Australia Council, and the casts and crews of the Canberra Youth Theatre and Toe Truck productions.

THE CHARACTERS

GILLIAN, 16, a schoolgirl

BRONWYN, 20, her sister

WENDY,

MONICA, } 16, GILLIAN's school friends

LYNETTE,

TONY, 19, a rock musician

BIGGLES, 28, a dermatologist adventurer and BRONWYN's boyfriend

DEREK, 16, his brother

KAREN, 16, a schoolgirl

ADAM, 16, her boyfriend

MUM, DAD, and other SCHOOLKIDS

Back row: Antoinette Blaxland (BRONWYN), *Nici Wood (Director of the Toe Truck production), Meredith Phillips* (WENDY/KAREN), *Andrew Lloyde* (TONY, ADAM, BIGGLES, DEREK), *Anna Yates* (LYNETTE/MONICA). *Front row: Fiona Stewart* (GILLIAN), *Dummies* (MUM/DAD/OTHER KIDS). *Photo: Sandy Edwards*

DAGS

GILLIAN *is dressed in pyjama bottoms and a sloppy-joe, a paper bag with holes cut out for the eyes is on her head. She is speaking to her imaginary audience.*

GILLIAN: I guess you're all wondering why I've got this paper bag on my head. It's cos I'm ugly. Hideous, A whole lot of you are probably thinking 'The paper bag's a pretty melodramatic stunt.' And that's true, I s'pose. I'm a pretty melodramatic sort of person. But that doesn't mean I'm not ugly too.

She takes off the paper bag and inspects it.

I thought it'd be okay if I cut out these eyeholes. But I didn't account for the noise problem. The paper crackles when I breathe in and out. Oh well…

She tosses the paper bag away.

GILLIAN *is in her room. She walks towards the bed and begins inspecting her face as if in a mirror. She sighs hopelessly. She continues to speak to her imaginary audience.*

GILLIAN: I felt *so* crummy this morning I couldn't face going to school. Full-scale ack-attack—face like a relief map of Switzerland, you know.

She flops face down, head buried on the bed. She lifts her head wearily to speak again.

Mum said I had to go to school. [*Mimicking* MUM] 'Don't be ridiculous, Gillian. No one's impressed by your drama queen performance.'

She collapses again, groaning, then rolls onto her back to face the ceiling.

Errgghh… why am I such a pathetic human being?

There is a thump! thump! on the door.

BRONWYN: [*outside the door*] Gillian!

GILLIAN *groans and buries her head again.*

Mum! She's locked herself in again!

GILLIAN: Leave me alone!

BRONWYN: You can't stay in there all day and night like a vegetable. Why don't you get off your big fat bum and set the table for Mum.

GILLIAN: All *right!* I will in a sec.

[*To her audience*] That bellowing witch out there is my sister Bronwyn.

BRONWYN *appears in an immaculate running suit. As* GILLIAN *speaks,* BRONWYN *runs on the spot, touches her toes, generally goes through her paces with polished ease. She takes off the tracksuit, and folds it up precisely and neatly. Then, in her underwear, she inspects her body in a mirror with detached, almost professional interest.*

Bronwyn's a really motivated person. She's doing a Communications course at tech at night even though she works all day in the florist shop. Bronwyn says 'No one's going to hand you a great life on a silver platter'… um, or something like that. Anyway, she reckons you can't slob around whingeing about things. Like I do. And she never has chipped nail polish or split ends or anything. That's the sort of person she is.

BRONWYN: Gillian! Do I have to come in there and drag you off that bed?

GILLIAN *groans and heaves herself off the bed.*

GILLIAN: I'm going!

[*To audience*] Bronwyn's not really stoked on having a little sister that's a vegetable.

GILLIAN *slouches out to the dining roam.*

I guess I'd better introduce the rest of my wonderful family.

GILLIAN *hoists a dummy of a middle-aged woman into one of the dining chairs, and props her at the table.*

Mum. Poor old Mum. It's not her fault I'm such a hopeless case. She sighs a lot and looks worried.

She demonstrates, using the dummy.

She's a very tired person basically.

She slumps the dummy face forward on the table, as if exhausted.

I would be too if I worked as hard as she does and had to be married to Dad. I used to try and talk over my problems with Mum.

GILLIAN *sits the dummy up again and rests her head on its shoulder like a child being comforted.*

But the more I told her about how crazy and miserable I feel, the more worried she'd look.

GILLIAN *mock weeps and clutches the dummy.*

Oh Mum… what am I going to do… I'm so fat and ugly.
[*Mimicking* MUM] 'If you're so convinced you're ugly, you'll just have to develop a lovely personality to make up for it, won't you.'

GILLIAN *drops the dummy back in its chair hopelessly.*

Terrific. So I've got a lousy personality as well. Sympathy's never been Mum's forte. She means well though.

GILLIAN *hoists a male dummy into another chair.*

There's not much to say about Dad. Bronwyn and me call him The Black Hole. 'Cos he's this dirty great mass of nothing sucking energy out of everything around him. If you hear someone sucking their teeth or grunting occasionally, you'll know it's Dad.

GILLIAN *flings a cloth over the table. She turns on the TV and then has to shout over the sound of a burbling game show. She turns the heads of the dummies to face the TV.*

We always have the telly on at dinnertime, so it's not so obvious no one's talking.

GILLIAN *takes her place at the table, staring sullenly at the tablecloth.* BRONWYN *strides in and scowls at the TV noise.*

BRONWYN: Do we have to have that thing on all the time?

BRONWYN *switches the TV off and sits down too.*

What's wrong with some family communication at the dinner table?

GILLIAN switches out of her withdrawn sulk for a moment.

GILLIAN: Bronwyn's big on communication.

GILLIAN and BRONWYN eat. BRONWYN scowls at her plate.

BRONWYN: I told you not to give me so much potato, Mum.

BRONWYN looks at MUM and DAD staring blankly, then puts down her knife and fork to make an announcement.

I think it's time this family had a discussion about Gillian's problem.

Silence. GILLIAN doesn't look up from her plate. BRONWYN is exasperated by the lack of response from MUM and DAD.

You admit you've got a problem, don't you Gillian.

GILLIAN still hangs her head.

See! She won't even answer me.

GILLIAN: It's none of your business.

BRONWYN: Oh, but it *is* my business. I've gotta put up with you moping and slobbing round the house all the time.

GILLIAN: I'll try to cry more quietly.

BRONWYN: Oh God, listen to it. Sniff, sniff. The drama queen's off again. She's—

GILLIAN: Shutup Bronwyn.

BRONWYN: Look Mum, Gilly needs help. She's got no friends at school or—

GILLIAN: I've got friends!

BRONWYN: [*snorting*] I wouldn't call hanging round with a couple of deadbeats no one else will talk to, 'friends'.

GILLIAN slumps back, defeated.

And she's never been out with boys. She's sixteen for Chrissake. I mean, most sixteen year olds have boyfriends and—

GILLIAN jumps up.

GILLIAN: Shutup Bronwyn! You just shutup! Did anyone ever tell you you're a disgusting bitch?

GILLIAN runs out howling. BRONWYN watches her go, sighs and shakes her head.

BRONWYN: [*to* MUM] See what I mean?

> GILLIAN *hurls herself face down onto her bed, heaving and hiccupping with sobs. After a moment, sniffing, she lifts her head.*

GILLIAN: Bronwyn reckons people don't want to know you if you're a misery-guts. She reckons people respond to 'positive energy'. Which means things are looking lousy for me…

> GILLIAN *sighs, then like a released spring, jumps up and gets a Mars bar from her schoolbag. She keeps talking, nibbling on the Mars bar.*

What really gets me—oh, excuse me eating—what gets me is that everyone says 'Oh, adolescence is this really terrible, painful time', but if any kid—like me for example—wants to lie around being miserable for a couple of years, they all say 'What's wrong with you? You've got everything going for you. Stop feeling sorry for yourself.' Like you should be romping around being a joyous little teenager like in some Yank TV show. You gotta admit, it isn't logical. Oh, *Gillian.* Pig, pig, pig! Stop stuffing your face.

> *She grabs the wrist holding the Mars bar as if the hand belongs to someone else. In a tug of war with that hand, she drags herself over to stuff the Mars bar away under the mattress. Then she sits on her hands on the bed, to control herself.*

Self-control, Gillian.

Seeing me pig out like that, you all probably think 'It's her fault she's so fat and hideous.' Which is a fair enough thing to think.

> GILLIAN *sits for a moment, rigid with an effort of self-control. Suddenly she gasps out with relief.*

Oh, it's hopeless.

> *She grabs the Mars bar again and takes a bite with delicious relief.*

Aagghh… why fight it.

> *She flops flat on her back on the bed.*

Some mornings when I wake up and remember it's a school day, it's like I'm paralysed.

After a moment of 'paralysis', GILLIAN heaves herself up off the bed and starts changing into a school uniform.

I get this sick feeling—right here in my guts—when I think about facing all the kids at school. I admit it's not usually *that* bad when I get there. But it's bad enough. What Bronwyn says about me and school is sort of true. I don't really have any proper friends there.

The schoolyard. GILLIAN *strolls in. Several dummies of girls and boys in school uniform are sitting around the yard, as if chatting in groups. Live girls, also in school uniform, are chatting to the dummies.*

GILLIAN: You might've forgotten what it's like. But the thing to remember is that kids are *vicious* to each other.

She walks around the dummies like a dispassionate wildlife commentator.

They spend most of their time ripping each other apart, ganging up on weak kids, playing musical boyfriends and all that stuff. Not my idea of a fun way to spend your adolescence. I stay out of it now. But I *used* to have friends. Like Wendy.

GILLIAN *flops down on her tummy in an open area.* WENDY *comes to flop down beside her, chummily.*

Wendy was my *best* friend.

WENDY: Do you reckon we'll still be friends when we leave school and everything?

GILLIAN: Ooh yeh.

WENDY: 'Cos my sister reckons she stopped seeing all her old friends when she left.

GILLIAN: Yeh but she's—

WENDY: Oh, wouldn't it be awful not to know any of your school friends later on. Even when I'm really old I want to have all these amazing friends I've known for ages. 'Cos by then we'll all be doing really fascinating things and we'll want to be able to say 'Oh, I've known Gillian for—ooh, let me see—twenty years.'

GILLIAN: We will. We just have to make an effort to—

WENDY *sits up suddenly, speaking fervently.*

WENDY: We have to, Gilly! We have to make the effort.

GILLIAN: No worries, Wendy. Calm down.

Both girls roll onto their backs, lying in the grass, chatting.

Wendy and me'd talk for hours.

WENDY: Rivka Berman reckons her mother could *tell* when she lost her virginity.

GILLIAN: Yeh but Rivka Berman's mother's a looney. A real space cadet.

WENDY: I'm serious, Gillian. I mean, like, what if there's something *different* about you—after you do it—and your mother can *tell*.

GILLIAN: My mother wouldn't realise my head was ripped off till I didn't eat all my dinner.

WENDY: Like maybe you sort of exude something that says 'I've done it'—that mothers can *see*.

GILLIAN: Aww, bullshit. Old wives' tales. I wouldn't worry Wendy.

WENDY: My mother knows *heaps* of things I don't tell her.

GILLIAN: That's because you're a crummy liar.

WENDY: You think about Tanya Gilchrist. We could *tell* she was sleeping with guys.

GILLIAN: [*laughing*] Yeh but that was because she was mincing round with her Pill packet half hanging out of her pocket.

But WENDY *is still worried, deep in thought.*

WENDY: I dunno. Maybe it's like a biological change that mothers pick up by *instinct*. Hormonal… yeh, maybe it's hormones.

GILLIAN *stands up.* WENDY *goes over and gathers together a huddled group of girls around her.* GILLIAN *speaks to the audience.*

GILLIAN: Okay—so Wendy isn't all that bright. But she was my best friend. One problem with Wendy was that she was always wanting to be in a *group*. A clique. I could never see why we needed to have some clique of goony girls to hang around with, but I went along with it.

GILLIAN *takes her place in the circle of chatting girls.* WENDY *is being theatrical, holding the floor.*

WENDY: Oh *God*—have you seen that new Economics teacher? [*In a mock snobby voice*] Mr Stenson-Smythe, have you seen the way he walks? [*Demonstrating*] He kind of sticks his bum out and wiggles it.

LYNETTE *laughs a little too enthusiastically.*

It wasn't that funny, Lynette.

LYNETTE *immediately feels very foolish.* WENDY *pulls a face about* LYNETTE—*that she's a dag.* WENDY *takes two of the dummies by the arm and, whispering conspiratorially to them, walks a few feet away to form a new huddled group. Left alone with* GILLIAN, LYNETTE *watches* WENDY *go with a mournful, vulnerable stare.*

GILLIAN: [*to audience*] The whole 'group' business seemed to be about who got snubbed and bitched about this week.

GILIIAN *gives* LYNETTE *an awkward smile.*

WENDY: Hey, Gilly—can you come here for a sec?

GILLIAN *jerks another apologetic smile to* LYNETTE *and goes over to join* WENDY.

GILLIAN: How come you've left Lynette over—
WENDY: We have to save you from getting stuck with her.
GILLIAN: I didn't mind being—
WENDY: We're all really sick of Lynette. I mean, she says such daggy things. And she laughs like a pig. It's so embarrassing sometimes.

WENDY *moans theatrically as* LYNETTE *starts walking towards the group.*

Oh *God*, she's coming over here. Well, I'm not going to talk to her.

LYNETTE *joins the group, as* GILLIAN *walks away from the others.*

GILLIAN: I knew it was only a matter of time before I was the odd girl out.

GILLIAN *turns back to see* LYNETTE *and* WENDY *sniggering bitchily together.*

WENDY: Gillian's just incredibly immature for her age.
LYNETTE: Oh yeh, she's so *young*. Young in the head.

WENDY: Some people just mature earlier than other people.

LYNETTE: [*sniggering*] Obviously. I never liked her. But I thought you really liked her.

WENDY: Oh, you know, you go through stages—silly, immature stages. It's terribly embarrassing when you grow out of someone though.

GILLIAN *sighs painfully.*

GILLIAN: Okay—so I was crazy to put up with it. But everyone did. And Wendy was my best friend.

As GILLIAN *keeps talking,* LYNETTE *and the dummies dissappear.* WENDY *comes over to* GILLIAN *and does a few things to tart her up for a night out—lipstick, make-up etc.* GILLIAN *stands limply while* WENDY *makes the changes.*

Wendy's next 'stage' was what she called 'going hunting'. For guys, that is.

[*To* WENDY] Aww, Wendy, I'll have to lie to Mum and Dad again. And we're under age.

WENDY: Don't be a wimp, Gilly. What else can we do?

At the rock gig. As rock music starts up WENDY *drags the reluctant* GILLIAN *into a dim area with flashing dance floor lights.*

GILLIAN: I don't even like rock gigs.

WENDY *and* GILLIAN *pick up drinks and perch on stools.* GILLIAN *looks very awkward, slouching and grim-faced.* WENDY *is very posed, self-conscious, eyes scanning the room sharply.*

WENDY: Don't turn around fast or anything. But there are a couple of guys near the smokes machine staring at us. Oh, one of them's alright looking. Oh God, Gillian—try and look a little bit awake.

While WENDY *checks out the talent,* GILLIAN *turns grimly to the audience for a moment.*

GILLIAN: I worked out pretty soon that Wendy was only using me as a stooge. She wanted to drag a doggy-looking friend like me around so she'd always be the spunky one. Guys'd check us out and draw straws to see who got the spunk and who got the dumpy ugly one.

[*To* WENDY] Can we go home, Wendy?

WENDY: We only just got here, Gillian.

GILLIAN: It's so loud. Last time my ears were ringing for two days. Maybe I should go home and you can—

WENDY Don't be crazy, I can't stay here on my own. Oh! There he is. I know he doesn't look much just standing there but when he gets up on that stage behind that guitar, he's absolutely gorgeous.

WENDY *starts bopping on her stool enthusiastically, eyes fixed adoringly on the stage.*

GILLIAN: This is when the trouble really started between Wendy and me. Tony. Gorgeous Tony. Bass player with a fourth-rate garage band that know five chords between them with a pimply lead singer with a phoney Cockney accent. We had to go and see Tony's crummy band every week so Wendy could bat her eyelids at him.

WENDY: I've never actually seen him with anyone who looks like a girlfriend. Gilly, he's walking over this way! Oh… I feel sick… shit, I won't be able to *speak.*

A cool, gelled, slow-witted young man, strolls over smugly.

TONY: Hi. I've seen you at a few other gigs.

WENDY: Oh, I really like the music. The band's great.

TONY: Oh—ta.

WENDY *grins coyly,* TONY *grins back at her.* GILLIAN *turns to the audience and rolls her eyes sarcastically.*

What's wrong with your friend?

WENDY: Gillian? [*Giggling*] What's wrong with you, Gilly?

WENDY *giggles, eager to please* TONY.

GILLIAN: I'll just go to the loo.

TONY: You do that.

As GILLIAN *walks away,* WENDY *and* TONY *settle into an inaudible conversation.* WENDY *squirms coyly and* TONY *struts and poses cockily as they chat each other up.* GILLIAN *watches them from a distance for a moment.*

GILLIAN: Tony's no intellectual giant. In fact, he's solid concrete north of the necktie. But Wendy was rapt in him.

◆ ◆ ◆ ◆

The schoolyard. GILLIAN *finds a spot on a bench to flop down.*

GILLIAN: All Wendy could talk about was Tony. Tony said this or that, Tony blah blah blah.

WENDY *wanders over to join* GILLIAN, *talking about* TONY *all the way.*

WENDY: Tony reckons I'm really old for my age. Like, he says he'd never have guessed I'm only 16. [*Giggling rapturously*] You know what he said the other day? I said 'How much do you really like me?' And he said [*Mimicking* TONY] 'Aww—I don't mind ya.' [*Giggling*] Can you believe it?

GILLIAN: Amazing.

WENDY: [*suddenly serious*] Of course, I realise Tony's music is very important to him. I'll have to fit in with it. I'd never ask him to choose between me and music.

GILLIAN: Sure. But maybe you shouldn't let—

WENDY: Ooh—it's nearly three o'clock! [*Jumping up*] I've gotta meet Tony. [*Rapt*] He's gonna let me sit in on rehearsal.

WENDY *runs off, leaving* GILLIAN *sitting alone and glum.*

GILLIAN: I guess it'd be melodramatic to say Wendy dropped me for Tony. But, let's face it, she dropped me for Tony. The only time I ever saw her anymore was when something was going wrong.

WENDY *and* TONY *are having a fight.* WENDY *is teary and shrill,* TONY *is sullen.*

WENDY: Why didn't ya tell me you went out with her?

TONY: Who said I did?

WENDY: Aw, don't give me that shit, Tony. Heaps of people saw ya at the pub. And I'm not blind. I can see the lovebites on ya neck.

TONY *guffaws.* WENDY *sniffles.*

Oh Tony… I thought we were really rapt…

TONY: What did you expect me to do on a Satday night?

WENDY: Wasn't my fault Mum wouldn't let me out.

TONY: Well, I dunno…

WENDY: She said I could go out this weekend.

TONY: I dunno.

WENDY: [*acidly*] Don't know much, do you? Why *her*? Did you sleep with her?

TONY *doesn't answer.*

I hate her guts. Why did you have to pick her? Well, she can keep ya. You deadshit, Tony Cropley!

WENDY *runs off crying to flop down beside* GILLIAN.

[*Sniffly*] Oh I dunno, Gilly—he says he really cares about me.

GILLIAN: It doesn't sound like it to me.

WENDY: He was really sorry. He even cried a little bit.

GILLIAN: Ha, that old routine.

WENDY: But I really *really* love him, Gilly.

GILLIAN: You can't act like a doormat.

WENDY: Ohhh… he's so sweet. You should've seen his face. He took my hand and he goes 'I really care about you, Wendy'. He's even gonna write a song about me.

GILLIAN: Wendy! I can't believe you're being taken in by this bullshit artist.

WENDY: Tony's not a bullshit artist! You've never liked him. 'Cos you're jealous. You just can't stand to see someone else in love. You're trying to break Tony and me up!

WENDY *flounces off.*

GILLIAN: She's probably right. Anyway, I finally decided to give up on Wendy. In fact, I decided to give up on friends and being a social success altogether. That was all ages ago—last year. Now I'm just a happy social cripple. I hang round with Monica now.

MONICA, *a dowdy, gauche, unself-conscious girl slouches in and sits beside* GILLIAN.

Monica isn't really a friend. More like an ally. A fellow cripple. Monica and me can get through a packet of Tim Tams in ten minutes flat. Truly.

MONICA *pulls a packet of Tim Tams out of her bag and they start munching on them.*

Do you have food orgasms?

MONICA *shrugs.*

I reckon I do. When I think about chocolate or something, I get food horny. And then when I eat it—whammo! Food orgasm. Is that what it's like for you?

MONICA: Dunno. Just like the taste.

GILLIAN *nods. They nibble in silence.*

GILLIAN: Did you go out on the weekend?

MONICA: Nuh. Mucked round at home.

GILLIAN: Would you rather have gone out?

MONICA: [*shrugging*] Could've gone ten pin bowling with my brother and his mates. Just as easy to stay home.

GILLIAN: Yeh, I guess…

More silent eating. GILLIAN *is deep in thought.* MONICA *is deep in Tim Tams.*

[*To audience*] Monica isn't a great conversationalist. Basically, we just sit together so it isn't so obvious we're alone. [*To* MONICA] Hey, do you ever get a kind of flash of what you'll be like in ten years or twenty years? What sort of person you'll be?

MONICA: Just older.

GILLIAN: Maybe not. Maybe you'll be really different. Like, you think about all the older people you know. I bet they didn't have any idea how they'd end up.

MONICA: Hunh?

GILLIAN: I mean, what if poor old Mum had realised how'd she'd end up. Frightening, isn't it, how wrong we might be about our own futures.

MONICA: [*in a matter-of-fact way, without deliberate pathos*] No big deal. It's obvious. I'll end up as Miss Lipton—'the fat one'. The only real choice is between teachers college or a 'go-ahead career in banking'. My brother reckons it's go-ahead. Pretty much the same either way. I guess I'll go round to my parents for Sunday dinner every week, go ten pin bowling once a week, save up for a holiday in Fiji once every three years. That's it.

GILLIAN: But Monica, that's so depressing—

MONICA: Why? I like bowling. I'm only kidding when I say I don't.

GILLIAN: What I really like about Monica is the way she's so laid back. She really doesn't worry about things. I'm hoping some of it'll rub off on me. [*To* MONICA] Do you ever worry that you might *never* get a boyfriend?

MONICA: All that stuff's overrated, Gillian.

GILLIAN: Oh yeh yeh, I know. But still—

MONICA: Look, have a look around.

> MONICA *waves her hand around the schoolyard.*

All those drooby guys. Would you wanna touch any of them with a ten foot pole?

GILLIAN: Ooh no.

MONICA: Right. Some of them might be okay if they're kept at the right temperature for a few years.

GILLIAN: But it'd be nice to think you *could* if you wanted. Be sure you were rejecting them and not—

MONICA: [*wearily patient*] Gillian. Do you really want to be like all of them?

GILLIAN: [*laughing*] Sex kittens and spunkrats. No thanks.

MONICA: Look at them all. Fretting themselves, getting worked up about who's going out with who, who's the best looking. All that posing. I couldn't be bothered.

GILLIAN: Nah…

MONICA: [*suddenly philosophical*] The way I see it, I'm developing qualities in myself that grow and improve with time. Not just good looks that wither and fade with age.

GILLIAN: That's fantastic, Monica—

MONICA: I just wouldn't want to be beautiful.

GILLIAN: Oh, neither would I.

MONICA: Think of the pressure. It'd be terrible. I'd hate to be gorgeous.

> KAREN, *a placid, pretty girl in a very short uniform and trendy haircut, parades past them, waving across to some friends.*

GILLIAN: Speaking of spunks… Bitch.

> GILLIAN *and* MONICA *follow* KAREN *with their eyes.*

Lucky bitch.

MONICA: Karen's not happy. I bet she's not.

GILLIAN: She looks pretty happy to me.

KAREN *approaches two boys in school uniform. One of the boys,* ADAM, *is good-looking and confident.* GILLIAN *and* MONICA *watch them flirting. There is obviously special attraction between* KAREN *and* ADAM.

Looks like Karen and Adam are getting together. I always expected that. They're like the King and Queen.

MONICA: Hunh?

GILLIAN: Well, she's the Star Sex Kitten of our year and he's the Head Heartbreaker, Chief Spunk. Royalty marrying royalty.

MONICA: I don't even think he's that attractive.

GILLIAN: Too full of himself. He catches the same bus as me, y'know.

MONICA: Yeh? Does he ever talk to you?

GILLIAN: You're kidding. He doesn't know I exist.

On the school bus. GILLIAN *is sitting on the bus, when* ADAM, *puffed from running, jumps on at the last minute.*

ADAM: [*to bus driver*] Thanks for waiting, mate.

ADAM *drops himself heavily into a seat a few rows in front of* GILLIAN *as the bus takes off.* GILLIAN *groans.*

GILLIAN: [*to audience*] imagine cruising through life *knowing* bus drivers are going to wait for you. And women are going to fall in love with you. I should hate someone like that. But I don't.

GILLIAN *sighs, bites her lip, strangles herself, groans, hams up having an internal battle.*

All right. I'm going to admit something I never thought I'd admit to *any*one *ever.*

I've got a crush on Adam.

Head over heels. Uncontrollable passion, etcetera, etcetera. Unrequited passion, of course. Now I know this sounds like I'm throwing away everything I've said so far. And I guess I am. I know every girl at school except Monica is in love with him. I know he'd never go for a dag like me. I know it's hopeless. I know all that. But I can't help it.

ADAM *turns his head to look at something out the bus window and almost looks straight at* GILLIAN, *oblivious to her.* GILLIAN *almost swoons.*

You see? Just thinking he might look at me, my heart starts pounding like mad. And then I worry about whether he can *tell* my heart's going crazy, and I have to act really cool. This crush—it's like a disease. Do you know—oh, I'm almost too embarrassed to admit this—Adam misses the bus sometimes. 'Cos he's chatting up some girl or something. And do you know what I do? I get off the bus after one stop and walk back to school, so I can hang round the bus stop hoping he'll turn up. Just so I can ride on the same bus with him. Isn't that the most pathetic thing you've ever heard?

ADAM *gets off the bus.* GILLIAN *looks deflated.*

Ohh... now it's like the whole day is over. No chance left. Who knows what I'm hoping will happen—that he'll throw himself at my feet right on the bus. I'm crazy.

GILLIAN'*s bedroom. She sits hunched up and brooding.*

GILLIAN: I can lie here for hours thinking about him. Writing these movies in my head where Adam and me are the stars. I try to imagine how he'd notice me and fall hopelessly in love with me and all that. Like, one of my favourites is that the bus breaks down one day in this remote place and there we are stranded together. He discovers that I was really this fascinating woman all along. Far more interesting than all those silly girls at school. *But*—I say that I can't bear to be just another notch on his belt. So Adam has to beg me to go out with him. Grovel almost. That's a pretty over-the-top version of—

A hearty voice booms outside the door.

BIGGLES: Whee-eere's that Gillian? Where's the big G-force?

GILLIAN: Oh-oh. Biggles.

BIGGLES *bursts into* GILLIAN*'s room and grabs* GILLIAN *in a hefty but playful wrestle hold.*

BIGGLES: Give in, G-force? Give in?

GILLIAN: Yes, yes. You're hurting me.

BIGGLES: You have to promise to arm-wrestle with me. Promise?

GILLIAN: Anything, anything.

BIGGLES *lets her go and positions himself to arm-wrestle with her.* BRONWYN *comes in, carrying two big bags, and watches them with faint annoyance.*

BRONWYN: I don't know why you bother. Gillian's incredibly unfit.

BIGGLES *pretends to be having terrible trouble getting* GILLIAN*'s arm down.* BRONWYN *and* GILLIAN *both roll their eyes at his antics.*

BIGGLES: Look at that! She's vicious. An arm of steel!

GILLIAN: Can I have my arm back please, Biggles?

BIGGLES *lets her go and ruffles her hair with rough affection.*

BIGGLES: 'Biggles'—I love it. She's a barrel of laughs your little sister, Bronwyn.

BRONWYN: Hysterical.

BIGGLES: [*noticing the bags*] Oh, you got the stuff out of the car. Beaudie! Little fashion parade for you, Gilly.

From the bags BRONWYN *and* BIGGLES *retrieve a set each of full scuba diving regalia. They dress up in the equipment over their clothes.*

GILLIAN: Biggles has been Bronwyn's boyfriend for the last six months. His real name's John or something. But I call him Biggles 'cos he's such a gung-ho type, and 'cos he likes me calling him that.

By day, he's a mild-mannered dermatologist, but every weekend he and Bronwyn take up some new amazingly dangerous hobby. They don't go on dates—they go on adventures, expeditions, *jumps*. They go on five day hikes and climb mountains and throw themselves down big holes in the ground on ropes for some reason. Bloody loony if you ask me.

Biggles is one of those disgusting people who's terrific at everything, even if he's never done it before. He wins fun runs, lifts weights, flies planes, skis like a champion, scores 200 at ten-pin bowling, sails and knits. He knits these fantastic jumpers.

Enough to make you sick. But don't get me wrong. I actually like old Biggles a lot, even if he can't do anything about my acne. He's always been nice to me. Nicer than Bronwyn for sure. He made me go aerobatic flying with him once—you know, loop-the-loop and all that terrifying stuff. He didn't even mind when I threw up all over him in his new flying suit.

BIGGLES *and* BRONWYN *pose for* GILLIAN *in the scuba gear.*

BIGGLES: Da da!

GILLIAN: You're going scuba diving.

BIGGLES: You guessed! Wanna come? We could still squeeze you in the scuba course.

GILLIAN: I don't know how to do it.

BRONWYN: Neither do we. It's a beginner's course. We thought it'd be fun to try it. Come with us.

GILLIAN: Oh no, I'd be too scared. I'd feel like I couldn't breathe or—

BIGGLES: Don't be a chicken!

He leaps onto the bed and squeezes GILLIAN *tightly. She is limp in his beefy grip.*

It's not scary once they teach you how. We could buddy-breathe, Gillo! How about that!

BIGGLES *tries to buddy-breathe with her, transferring the mouthpiece to her and back again.* GILLIAN *giggles and fights him off.*

GILLIAN: Don't! I'd hate it! I'd panic!

BIGGLES: [*wrestling her*] You'd love it! Excitement! Adventure!

BRONWYN: Leave her alone, John. She obviously doesn't want to.

BIGGLES *stands up, regains his breath, straightens up his gear.*

BIGGLES: I don't get it, G-force. What's so great about staying home and—

BRONWYN: She wouldn't get up off her bum and do anything active.

She just wants to stay home feeling sorry for herself. Sulking.

BIGGLES: You unhappy about something, Gillo?

BRONWYN: She's just being selfish and lazy and unmotivated. She thinks the world's against her and she's hard done by.

BIGGLES: Yeh? You've got everything going for you, mate. [*Tickling her*] Beauty, brains, the offer of a lifetime to learn scuba diving. What more could you want?

GILLIAN *pushes him off for real this time, sulky.*

GILLIAN: I don't like being tickled, Biggles.

BIGGLES *backs off, puzzled.* GILLIAN *hangs her head.* BRONWYN *softens a little.*

BRONWYN: She's worried about never going out with boys.

BIGGLES: Yeh? I don't know what's wrong with those guys. I'd go for you—if Bron didn't already have her eye on being Mrs Dermatologist.

BRONWYN *flashes him a sharp look.* GILLIAN *tries to stifle a giggle and* BIGGLES *winks at her chummily. When he notices* BRONWYN's *steely look he changes the subject.*

What about my little brother then?

BRONWYN: I'm not sure that Derek is Gillian's type.

BIGGLES: He's all right. I'd admit he's not as gorgeous as I am and he's a bit of a wimp. But Derek's an intellectual type like you, Gillo.

BRONWYN: Yes, Gillian—why don't you stop whingeing and go out with Derek.

GILLIAN: Well, apart from the fact that he hasn't asked me—

BIGGLES: I can fix that.

GILLIAN: I don't *want* to go out with *any* guys.

BRONWYN: [*growling in frustration*] Ohh, you don't want anyone to help you. Enjoy your misery, misery-guts. C'mon, John.

BRONWYN *drags* BIGGLES *out.*

BIGGLES: I hate to see ya unhappy, Gillo.

GILLIAN *flops back on her bed dismally.*

GILLIAN: He's too good for Bronwyn.

◆   ◆   ◆   ◆

The schoolyard. ADAM *and a couple of dummies sit chatting.* GILLIAN *walks into the schoolyard to join* MONICA *in their usual spot.*

GILLIAN: There are so many things you have to keep track of that Monica and me have this system of making up a list at the beginning of the week.

> GILLIAN *sits with* MONICA. *Both girls scribble in notepads with one hand while with the other, they dip spoons into a huge gelato bucket between them, and suck the gelato off.* GILLIAN *is acutely aware of* ADAM*'s presence several yards away and glances across from time to time.*

MONICA: Right. You read yours out.

GILLIAN: Okay. Things I Must Remember To Do.

One—buy biros.

Two—get Mum's birthday present.

Three—be more patient with Bronwyn.

Four—be more assertive.

Five—eat less—Ohh, who am I kidding? Look at me feeding my face.

Why am I always eating till I feel sick?

This is revolting.

MONICA: Yeh, we definitely should've got the strawberry.

GILLIAN: No, *I'm* revolting. You know, sometimes when I'm walking along I accidentally see my reflection in a shop window and I think 'Who's that big blob of fat walking along?' And then I think 'Right. I'm gonna go on a savage diet.'

MONICA: It's bad for you. Dieting does terrible things to your body.

GILLIAN: It makes you thin. That's the whole idea, Monica.

MONICA: Give up. It's the food curse.

GILLIAN: Eh?

MONICA: We've both got it. The curse says you have to spend every single moment of your life thinking about food, craving it. But the curse also says you're never allowed to enjoy one scrap of it. You try to shove the food in and swallow it really fast, as if it's going to do less damage that way. But you still end up feeling contaminated— like it's a hunk of poison in your guts.

GILLIAN: Contaminated. Yeh, yeh…

KAREN *walks by with an easy grace and waves across to* ADAM.
He flicks his head for her to come over.

MONICA: Speaking of feeling sick.

GILLIAN: I thought you didn't let spunks worry you.

MONICA: There's something about Karen that really gets me.

GILLIAN: Look at her—like a lapdog. She shouldn't be at his beck and call like that. She should have more self-respect.

MONICA: You don't need self-respect when you look like that.

After a hello kiss, KAREN *sits on* ADAM'*s lap. They maul and nibble and chatter and giggle, watched by* GILLIAN *and* MONICA.

Errgghh… they're all over each other like a rash. Wouldn't you hate someone pawing at you like that?

GILLIAN: Oh yeh… horrible. Lots of people reckon Adam's really serious about Karen. Not just like all the others.

MONICA *shrugs and snorts dismissivey, then returns to the gelato.*

MONICA: You finished with this?

GILLIAN *nods limply.* MONICA *draws the gelato bucket closer, almost hugging it to herself, closed off from* GILLIAN. GILLIAN *keeps watching* ADAM *and* KAREN, *sighing painfully.*

GILLIAN: [*to audience*] I guess you're all thinking 'Why is she torturing herself?' I wish I knew the answer.

She gets up and walks out of the schoolyard.

It's a funny thing the way there's such a difference between your rational brain and your looney brain. My rational brain says, 'It's hopeless, Gillian, and you wouldn't want a conceited dickhead like Adam anyway. Don't torture yourself.' But I'm buggered if I can convince my looney brain about that.

The school bus. GILLIAN *takes a seat.* ADAM *runs and takes a seat as the bus starts up.* GILLIAN *pulls a book out of her bag and tries to concentrate on it, but she keeps glancing up at* ADAM. *Suddenly there's*

a grinding and clunking noise and the bus stops jerkily, jolting GILLIAN *and* ADAM.

ADAM: Shit—what was that?

ADAM *jumps up to see what's happening, craning his neck to watch what's going on at the front of the bus.*

Sounds like the pistons have shot through the head. Are we stuck here?

ADAM *stomps around, swearing under his breath.* GILLIAN *stares at the audience in shock for a moment.*

GILLIAN: I can't believe this. But I should point out that this is not a fantasy sequence. This is really happening. And I didn't sabotage the bus. Here we are—stranded right near the end of the bus route, so there's only me and Adam left on the bus. Now it's actually happened, I'm terrified. He'll probably just ignore me anyway. Stay calm, Gillian.

ADAM: Shit, the bloody bus prob'ly runs on mice and elastic bands. Did one of the bands break?

GILLIAN: [*timidly*] You might as well start walking.

ADAM: Yeh, this old wreck's stuffed.

ADAM *storms off the bus.* GILLIAN *tentatively follows him.*

Fan-bloody-tastic.

GILLIAN *and* ADAM *find themselves standing by the side of the road together, awkwardly.*

How are you anyway, Gillian?

GILLIAN: Okay.

ADAM *slams his fist angrily into his palm.*

ADAM: Can you believe it about that bomby bus? Shit.

GILLIAN: I'm used to it. This is the third bus I've been on that's broken down so far this year.

ADAM: Well, it's never happened to me before.

GILLIAN: No, it wouldn't have.

ADAM: Sorry?

GILLIAN: Nothing

ADAM *is rather awkward with her. Uneasily, he fills the silence.*

ADAM: Look… um… do you wanna start walking home? There won't be another bus for—

GILLIAN: Three-quarters of an hour.

ADAM: Shit. We definitely better start walking.

They start strolling, not too close together. ADAM *is polite, distracted.*

Are you… um… getting worried about the exams?

GILLIAN: Not too worried yet.

ADAM: No, well, you don't need to worry, do you.

GILLIAN: What do you mean?

ADAM: Well, you work hard—

GILLIAN: [*dismally*] Yeh, I'm the boring swot.

ADAM: Oh but you're smart too. One of the brightest in our year. I noticed that in English.

GILLIAN: [*muttering*] Yeh yeh, I'm the sensitive bookworm type.

ADAM: Sorry?

GILLIAN: Forget it.

ADAM: [*with new fervour*] Are you friends with Karen at all?

GILLIAN: Oh… um, not friends really. I mean, I *like* her, but we've never hung round together.

ADAM: But do you reckon you'd understand the way her mind works?

GILLIAN: Karen and I are pretty different people.

ADAM: Yeh but… oh shit… I dunno…

GILLIAN *shows a grimace of terror and indecision.*

GILLIAN: Are you and Karen… umm… having problems?

ADAM: We've been going round for a while now, right, and I really like her—I mean, I'm rapt in her—but… ohh… Do you mind me blabbing on about this?

GILLIAN: No, not at all.

ADAM: And you won't say anything to Karen or anyone?

GILLIAN: No way.

ADAM: Thanks.

GILLIAN: What's the problem?

ADAM: I wish Karen'd *say* more. She just *sits* there and I never know what she's thinking.

GILLIAN: Have you tried asking her?

ADAM: Oh yeh, and then she says I'm pressuring her.

GILLIAN: Maybe she's scared you'll think that what she's thinking is dumb.

ADAM: That's crazy! I don't care what she's thinking as long as I know what it is.

GILLIAN: That doesn't stop her feeling self-conscious.

ADAM: [*laughing*] Maybe she's not thinking anything at all and that's the problem.

GILLIAN: I'm sure that's not true, Adam.

ADAM: [*growling in exasperation*] Oh I dunno, Karen and I don't have anything to *talk* about. Like, when I go out with her, we just sit there not saying anything. So I kiss her and feel her up all the time so it's not so obvious that we don't talk.

GILLIAN: Look, I really think Karen's probably insecure. You haven't been going round all that long and, if you don't mind me saying so, you haven't exactly got a great record for staying with the same girl.

ADAM *grins cockily.* GILLIAN *laughs, relaxing a little.*

Adam The Heartbreaker.

ADAM: But Karen knows it's different with her.

GILLIAN: Give her more time and lots of security. When she trusts you more, I bet she'll open up.

ADAM: You reckon?

GILLIAN: Well, I don't *know* of course. But I reckon that's the best way for you to handle it.

ADAM: [*cheered up*] Yeh. Yeh it is. 'Cos there's no way I want to give her up. Oh—this is my place.

They stop. GILLIAN *looks awkwardly hopeful.*

Well—thanks for talking to me, Gillian. I feel much better, I really do. I hope you don't mind me—

GILLIAN: Oh no, it's fine.

ADAM: See you tomorrow or something.

GILLIAN: Yeh. Bye.

ADAM *goes off.* GILLIAN *stands, stunned.*

My whole body's numb. This is what it felt like the night I took a couple of Auntie Lorraine's Serepax.

You idiot, Gillian. Heaps of times, I've imagined my first real conversation with him. And when it really happens, I bugger it up! Then again, he really did open up to me. So maybe he talked about Karen the whole time. At least it's a start.

GILLIAN *staggers home in a dopey spin.*

GILLIAN'*s bedroom.*

BRONWYN *watches as* GILLIAN *tumbles onto her bed.*

BRONWYN: Are you all right, Gillian?

GILLIAN: No!

BRONWYN: What's up?

GILLIAN *sits up to address the audience.*

GILLIAN: I told her. All about my crush. I had to tell someone. Keeping things bottled up inside gives you ulcers. And anyway, Bronwyn's no idiot when it comes to male/female relations. She's been through the mill with guys and you can have a pretty good conversation with her about that stuff.

BRONWYN *perches on the edge of* GILLIAN'*s bed. They are in the middle of a heart-to-heart talk.*

BRONWYN: Karen Battley… I think I know the one you mean. An amazing looking girl. Perfect skin.

GILLIAN: Like a doll.

BRONWYN: [*laughing*] So beautiful and *so* boring. And he reckons she doesn't speak?

GILLIAN: She giggles a lot.

BRONWYN *laughs and shakes* GILLIAN *playfully.*

BRONWYN: Then what are you worried about, Gilly? If she's a boring mindless spunk, you've got a great chance to get this Adam guy. Go for it.

GILLIAN: [*falling face forward*] It's hopeless.

BRONWYN: [*deep in scheming*] Now let's plan this… I guess you are still a bit inexperienced—

BIGGLES: [*outside*] Bron! You ready, Bron?

BRONWYN: In here, darling!

BIGGLES bounds in wearing a snazzy parachute suit. He poses hammily for them.

BIGGLES: You like it?

BRONWYN: Tonight's just the theory lecture.

BIGGLES: I know, but I wanted to—y'know—get into the mood.

BRONWYN: [*to* GILLIAN] We're doing a skydiving course this week.

BIGGLES: We do our first jump on Saturday! Wanna come, Gillo?

BRONWYN: You know Gillian wouldn't want to.

BIGGLES: Still down in the dumps, huh? An arm-wrestle might cheer you up.

BRONWYN: Actually, Gillian and I are having a rather serious talk. If you could go and talk to Mum for a few minutes…

BIGGLES: Oh. Okey doke. How bout just a quick one?

He poses for an arm-wrestle with GILLIAN. BRONWYN *thumps him.*

BRONWYN: Out! Outside!

BIGGLES slinks out, waving goodbye to GILLIAN.

Now, the plan is—

GILLIAN: I don't want a 'plan'.

BRONWYN: I was thinking that since you've never been out with guys, you should maybe *practise* before you make a play for Adam.

GILLIAN: I don't like the sound of this plan, 'Make a play'? I don't want to be sneaky or—

BRONWYN: Go out with Derek. Practise on him.

GILLIAN: Yuk… you can't 'practise' on people. That's an awful idea.

BRONWYN: Do you want my help or not?

GILLIAN: Aww, Bronwyn…

BRONWYN: You might even like him.

GILLIAN: [*mumbling*] Oh all right…

BRONWYN: What was that?

GILLIAN: I said I'll do it.

BRONWYN: Great. I'll organise it.

> BRONWYN *runs out.* GILLIAN *pulls a horrified face. What has she let herself in for now?*

The following week. GILLIAN *is dressed for her date.*

GILLIAN: A blind date with Derek. Hmm, I don't know if I've done the right thing. If you think *I'm* a dag, you should see Derek. He was in my class all through primary school, then he went to the snotty boys' school up the road. In primary school, Derek was always the kid that everyone did nasty things to—you know, dog turds in his lunch and supaglue on his seat and sticking goony signs on his back. Stupid stuff like that. I felt sorry for him except he never fought back. He just looked back at everyone, going blink blink with his beady eyes. Apparently now he's the real whizz kid at his new school. But he's still a dag.

> GILLIAN *checks her appearance in the mirror.*

I thought it'd be best to meet on neutral ground.

> *The cinema centre. Derek is standing at the meeting place. He is stiff, gawky, pimply, spruced up in rather daggy clothes that don't quite fit.* GILLIAN *hangs back and watches him for a moment. Derek checks his watch. He adopts a 'relaxed' macho pose awkwardly, then shifts and tries another pose.*

Ohh no… if only he didn't try so hard. It's excruciating.

> GILLIAN *takes a deep breath and marches up to him. He almost jumps in fright.*

Derek. Hi.

DEREK: Oh hi, Gillian. How are you?

GILLIAN: Good thanks. I guess you're feeling a bit strange about this arranged marriage too.

DEREK: [*laughing nervously*] Oh well, it'll keep my brother and your sister off our backs.

GILLIAN: [*smiling*] Yeh.

> *There is an awkward silence.*

DEREK: Umm... have you got any preference about what movie you'd like?

GILLIAN: No, I'm not fussy.

DEREK: Well, let's see.

They step back and look up at the movie billboard.

GILLIAN: Oh, I've seen that one. It's a Yank weepie. You know, some good looking girl gets cancer. I cried a lot, I don't think you'd like it.

DEREK: I don't like Kung Fu movies.

GILLIAN: Neither do I. I'm not mad on car chase movies with 'zany humour'. But anything else would be fine. I'm not fussy.

DEREK: But there's only one movie left.

GILLIAN: I guess we see that one then.

GILLIAN and DEREK are at the movies. GILLIAN eats a choc-top icecream. They are both rigid with tension, staring straight ahead at the screen. A long breathless silence.

[*To audience*] I couldn't think of anything to say. It was crazy. There must have been heaps of things we could talk about. But the longer it went, the harder it got to get any words out. We watched *every* advertising slide like our lives depended on it. The Chinese restaurant round the corner from the movie theatre, Fays Frock Shop, group booking concessions, no smoking please.

Do you realise how hard it is to eat a choc-top without the person next to you hearing? And even with that slobbering noise, I could hear Derek *breathing* beside me. [*Shuddering*] Ugghh. I could hear him breathe out in relief when the movie started.

They watch the movie.

The movie was one of those American teenage slob comedies. You know, with gorgeous clear-skinned Prom Queens being chased by irresistible teenage hunks. If you think about it, it was a bit of a cruel joke that a couple of social cripples like Derek and me were watching a movie like that.

The movie sound suddenly lurches and whines; it has broken down. Derek swirls his head around wildly.

DEREK: What's happened?

GILLIAN: [*unsurprised*] The film's buggered.

DEREK: Isn't that amazing. I can't believe it broke down. I hope we get a refund.

GILLIAN: Things like this happen to me all the time.

The lights come up suddenly and brightly.

DEREK: I'm sorry, Gillian.

GILLIAN: Why? It's not your fault. I didn't like the film anyway.

DEREK: Mm—all that shouting and squealing—it was a bit juvenile. [*He tooks at his watch*] It's only 8.43. It's a bit early to—

GILLIAN: Yes, it's definitely too early to go home. Bronwyn'd give me heaps. What can we do?

DEREK: Oh… we could, um… [*Clearing his throat, then speaking as if he has rehearsed it*] how about we go back to my place?

GILLIAN: To your place? Where your parents live?

DEREK: I've got my own converted garage. Away from the house.

GILLIAN: Oh…

[*To audience*] This is probably completely crazy.

[*To* DEREK] Okay. Let's go. Got anything to munch at your place?

DEREK*'s garage. Fish tanks, a small computer, rubbish, piles of books and papers are scattered around.*

DEREK: This is where my brother John used to keep all his skiing stuff and rally bike and so on. When he moved out, Mum and Dad said I could fix it up and use it for my fish and my computer.

There are a couple of bean bags on the floor and they sit on them.

[*Laughing nervously*] But then Mum said I was such a slob she wouldn't clean up my room inside anymore, so I had to live out here. I like the privacy.

DEREK *shows a bit more life, as he sees a chance for humour. He guffaws.*

I'm such a slob there's even mushrooms growing out of the carpet over there. See?

GILLIAN *nods, looking faintly nauseated.* DEREK's *grin freezes and then crumbles as he realises his humour has fallen flat.*

GILLIAN: Did you say you had some chocolate?

DEREK *jumps up a little too quickly and starts rummaging through some junk.*

DEREK: Oh yeh. It's here somewhere—Fruit and Nut.

He unearths a crumpled ball of wrapper and looks inside it forlornly.

Oh. It *was* Fruit and Nut. Sorry, it's a bit squashy now.

He shows her the chocolate. GILLIAN *pulls a face.*

How about some coffee?

GILLIAN: Yeh, that'd be nice.

DEREK: [*babbling excitedly as he rummages again*] Yeh, coffee. I've got a jug and everything set up in here. Milk, milk, here we are.

He unearths a battered milk carton. He opens it and sniffs at it.

[*Suddenly desolate*] Oh—the milk's off.

GILLIAN: No milk? Well, don't worry. I won't—

DEREK: I could run up to the house and ask Mum to—

GILLIAN: Don't worry about it, Derek. Sit down and relax.

DEREK *is still hopping around nervously.*

DEREK: Yeh. Right.

Tensely, he 'relaxes' in the bean bag. An awkward silence follows, broken only by the slight rustle of bean bags and throat clearing.

GILLIAN: You've got an awful lot of fish.

DEREK: I breed tropicals.

GILLIAN: Uh huh.

Umm… is it hard to do? To breed them?

DEREK: Not most of them. But some [*he jumps up to point out a fish*] like this one, it's a very delicate business. See that red one? Well, according to one of my tropical breeders journals, that particular colouring is extremely rare everywhere except—oh, you're probably not that interested in fish breeding. It's fairly specialised stuff.

GILLIAN: It must be really interesting when you go right into it like you have.

> DEREK *leaps across to the computer.*

DEREK: Are you into computers?

GILLIAN: Not really.

DEREK: You shouldn't be scared of them.

GILLIAN: I'm not.

DEREK: [*babbling on*] There's really no reason to find computers frightening. It's just a matter of learning to understand them. To become computer-literate in the way we've always been word-literate.

Programming is really all about transferring things from here [*pointing to his head*] to here [*pointing to the computer*] and trying to—

GILLIAN: I'm not *scared* of computers. Just bored by them.

DEREK: Oh. Fair enough.

GILLIAN: Sorry, I didn't mean to…

DEREK: S'all right. It's easy to forget that the rest of the world isn't like a few egghead computer freaks in my maths class.

> GILLIAN *smiles encouragingly.*

Talking about computers makes me feel a bit more confident… y'know?

GILLIAN: I know. I'm nervous too though.

> DEREK *meets* GILLIAN'*s gaze directly and smiles, relaxing a little. He sits in the bean bag. They're next to each other, nervously aware of the other's physical presence.*

DEREK: [*panicky*] You don't play Dungeons and Dragons by any chance? 'Cos I've programmed the computer to—

> DEREK *stops when he sees* GILLIAN *shaking her head emphatically. Self-consciously,* DEREK *stretches out on the bean bag, virtually lying down. He's now a little closer to* GILLIAN.

GILLIAN: [*to audience*] I could see what might happen. Those moments when you're both aware of every tiny movement, but pretending you aren't. Waiting for the other person to make a definite move.

I could hear his breathing—almost panting with nerves. I'm quite fond of Derek. But I don't lust after him. No way. The only explanation I can offer is that I decided it was time to do *something* with *someone*. Even if it had to be with Derek. And I reckon Derek felt the same way. He didn't think I was sexy. He didn't care who I was. He was a desperate like me. Beggars can't be choosers and all that. Mutual exploitation.

> GILLIAN *leans onto one elbow, closer and facing* DEREK, *playing it cool. Both hold their breath and don't move an inch. Then they suddenly fall on each other in a feverish attempt at passionate kissing and mauling. A few moments of clumsy joyless grappling follow,* GILLIAN *and* DEREK *are half falling off the bean bags, squashing each other, limbs colliding, etc.*

Look, I don't mean to—

DEREK: This isn't working, is it.

> *They both collapse back on separate bean bags, defeated and panting.*

GILLIAN: Sorry Derek.

DEREK: S'all right, I feel better now. Relieved.

GILLIAN: Yeh, it's weird. I do too.

DEREK: I kept thinking I *ought* to, when I didn't really want to.

GILLIAN: Me too.

DEREK: Oh sorry—not that I'm saying you—

GILLIAN: It's okay, Derek. I don't find you attractive either.

> DEREK *laughs heartily for the first time.*

DEREK: It's very funny really.

> GILLIAN *can't help but splutter into laughter too.*

I was worried I was getting left behind. Missing out on something.

GILLIAN: Me too.

DEREK: By maybe we aren't missing out on anything so terrific anyway. I thought I had to make an effort—not to be such a hermit. I mean, up till now, I've worked on a system of keeping out of people's way. Other kids gave me a hard time at primary school.

GILLIAN: I remember. I feel rotten that I didn't stick up for you.

DEREK: How could you? It's vicious out there. It's every kid for himself.

GILLIAN: I don't know how you survived it.

DEREK: My survival technique was not to fight, keep a low profile, keep to myself…

GILLIAN: Has it worked?

DEREK: [*shrugging*] Not sure. I can't tell what I've missed. I've tried to make a definite point out of being different, odd. The odd boy with the fish and the computer. So people would think I *wanted* to be alone. And I suppose it was partly because of John.

GILLIAN: Biggles? I mean, your brother?

DEREK: You can't *compete* with a guy like him. How can you measure up against a brother who's good at everything. And *nice* too.

GILLIAN: Impossible. Hideous. Poor you.

A pause, as they are both deep in thought.

DEREK: Gillian, you won't… umm… tell anyone about tonight and how…

GILLIAN: Ooh no. In fact, maybe we should… you know…

DEREK: Make up a story between us?

GILLIAN *grins wickedly and nods.*

I suppose our little secret wouldn't do anyone any harm. And we'd both be let off the hook a bit.

GILLIAN: Beaudi, Derek. It's a deal.

The schoolyard. GILLIAN *walks in to join* MONICA. KAREN *and some dummies talk in a group in one corner.*

GILLIAN: [*to audience as she walks in*] Poor old Derek. There's something about him that makes even *me* feel like a sparkling social success.

GILLIAN *sits down beside* MONICA. MONICA *pulls a face.*

MONICA: Derek! I remember him from primary school. Errgghh, he's the kid who was always—

GILLIAN: That's the one. He's older now.

MONICA: Yuk. He's probably still a nutcase.

GILLIAN: Look Monica—

MONICA: You didn't kiss him did you?

GILLIAN: Well, actually—

MONICA: Oh *no*. Did he slip you the tongue?

GILLIAN: Slip me the—? Ugghh, that is the most disgusting expression—

MONICA: Did you cop his tongue or didncha?

GILLIAN: [*muttering as she turns away*] Sort of.

MONICA *scrambles round to face her.*

MONICA: Eh? Eh? What happened? I want *full details.*

GILLIAN: Monica, I never knew you were like this.

MONICA: My brother reckons there's a scale for measuring this stuff. Where did Derek get up to on the scale? Above the Waist Outside the Clothes? Below the Waist?

GILLIAN: [*dismally*] I really don't want to talk about this, y'know.

MONICA: [*nodding, a woman of the world*] You're pregnant.

GILLIAN: No! It wasn't anything like you're describing. It was kind of—

ADAM: Gillian! Hey Gillian—could you come over here for a sec?

GILLIAN *scrambles to her feet to hurry over to* ADAM.

MONICA: [*muttering*] Now who's a lap dog…

GILLIAN *and* ADAM *sit a little aside from everyone.* ADAM *is serious and thoughtful.*

ADAM: Sorry, Gillian—did I interrupt something?

GILLIAN: Oh no. Monica and I were just… you know…

ADAM: It's just that I find it easier to talk to you than anyone else, Gillian.

GILLIAN: You can talk stuff over with me any time, Adam.

ADAM: I've gotta cool off with Karen. Sometimes I feel like shaking her, yelling at her—try and get her to yell back at me. But she never does.

GILLIAN: That isn't how we decided you should handle it.

ADAM: I know. But I'm sick of hearing myself talk.

GILLIAN: Have you tried asking questions to get her talking about things she's interested in?

ADAM: What's she interested in? She doesn't do anything.

GILLIAN: That's not true, Adam. And anyway, if Karen's meant to be your girlfriend, that's a terrible way to—

ADAM: Don't get me wrong. I love her. I really care about her.

A big sigh is heard from ADAM *as he looks across to Karen.*

I dunno what to do. Sometimes I think she doesn't even *like* me much.

GILLIAN: Eh? Of course she does, Adam.

ADAM: She doesn't show it if she does.

GILLIAN: A lot of girls are really clever at hiding how much they like a guy.

ADAM: You think so?

GILLIAN: I know so.

ADAM: Thanks, Gillian. I always feel better after I talk to you.

ADAM *romps off to rejoin* KAREN, *cuddling her up to him.* GILLIAN *turns away.*

GILLIAN: It's enough to break your heart, isn't it?

GILLIAN *goes back to sit with* MONICA. MONICA *is cool and prickly with her.*

MONICA: You're crazy, y'know. Letting him tell you all his problems, turning you into a big salt-encrusted shoulder. Using you.

MONICA *turns slightly away, nibbling at something.*

GILLIAN: [*to audience*] Monica's partly right. But she was also pretty jealous. I never thought Monica and I had a proper friendship to get jealous about, but I guess I was wrong. Anyway, this business with Adam put a lot of strain on things with Monica. It became a regular event—Adam talking over The Karen Problem with me. Of course, it was excruciating for me, but I was sort of delirious. I admit I let things get out of hand. Adam thought it might be easier for him and Karen to talk if I came along on a date.

Okay, don't say it. I know this is looney. But I figured any chance to go out with him was worth it.

At the movies. GILLIAN, KAREN *and* ADAM *sit in a row, with* ADAM *in the middle.* ADAM *is leaning right over, arms round* KAREN, *kissing and mauling her.* GILLIAN *stares straight ahead at the screen, eating a choc-top.*

GILLIAN: It was the same teenage slob comedy I'd seen part of with Derek. So I was pretty bored.

ADAM *eventually comes up for air and turns to* GILLIAN.

ADAM: What do you think of the movie?

GILLIAN: Pretty crummy. Rather juvenile actually.

ADAM: Yeh, you're right.

GILLIAN: I don't much like Americans.

ADAM: Nah, not these sort of Americans for sure. There's some comedy stuff the Yanks do well—like *The Blues Brothers*.

GILLIAN: Yeh, I loved *The Blues Brothers* too!

ADAM *dives down again on* KAREN. GILLIAN *is left with the smile fading on her face. She fixes her eyes on the movie again.*

How the hell did I get into this?

ADAM *pops up again.*

ADAM: [*waving his hand at the screen*] It's not even very realistic. I bet it's not like that in college in America.

GILLIAN: Course not. These comedies are all the same anyway— formula stuff.

ADAM: Formula, yeh—that's right.

ADAM *swoops on* KAREN *again.* GILLIAN *sighs deeply.*

GILLIAN: I had to bite the inside of my cheek so I wouldn't cry. I hope Adam couldn't tell. Sometimes my face goes all red and blotchy when I'm about to cry.

The lights come up suddenly. ADAM *sits up again.*

ADAM: Is it over? I missed the end. What happened, Gillian?

GILLIAN, *on the verge of tears, jumps up.*

GILLIAN: Sorry. I feel sick. I'll have to go. I think I'm gonna throw up.

GILLIAN *runs out.*

ADAM: Oh. Bye Gillian.

GILLIAN: Times like this, I feel like I'm in a glass bubble in the middle of a world full of people. I can see everyone but they don't really see me. I'm kind of separate, like I'm in another dimension or something. Even if I tapped on the glass and yelled out no one would hear.

> GILLIAN *is overcome by another wave of sobbing. She talks in teary staccato.*

It's hopeless. I'm ugly. I'm fat. I'm boring. No one wants to know me. *I* wouldn't want to know me either.

> *She whips herself up till she's heaving and gulping for air, beginning to hyperventilate.* BRONWYN *runs in with a paper bag which she holds over* GILLIAN*'s face.* GILLIAN*'s breathing gradually returns to normal.* BRONWYN *then rubs* GILLIAN*'s back soothingly.* GILLIAN *is limp and sniffly.*

BRONWYN: Shh, shh, calm down. C'mon, breathe deeply. Slowly. Gilly, why do you get yourself all worked up like this? It hurts me to see it, mate. It upsets Mum too. She's so worried, she's in there watching *Gilligan's Island*.

GILLIAN: [*wailing*] Ohh, Bronwyn, don't make me feel guilty too.

BRONWYN: Shh, settle down. I'm just saying we all worry about you, kiddo.

GILLIAN: Can you reach that packet of biscuits under there?

BRONWYN: Biscuits! Gillian—

> *Against her better judgement,* BRONWYN *drags a packet of biscuits out from under the bed.* GILLIAN *bites into one with delicious relief.*

How many more secret food stashes have you got?

GILLIAN: Just these. The biscuits shaped like little pillows. Always make me feel better.

BRONWYN: You can't keep using food to solve problems, Gilly.

GILLIAN: Don't be so logical, Bronwyn. This is a major disaster.

BRONWYN: You have a major disaster about once a week!

> *Pause.*

GILLIAN: She's right. One trauma after another. Sometimes I wonder whether I manufacture problems because I'm bored. Mum says I always was a drama queen.

GILLIAN *stops eating the biscuit, looks at it and pulls a face, as if it's suddenly turned sour.*

Even pillow biscuits can't cheer me up this time.

GILLIAN *topples back on the bed, wailing.*

It's hopeless. Don't waste your time on me, Bronwyn. This is rock bottom. I'm just a huge blob of nothing.

BRONWYN: You can't keep talking like that, mate. You've gotta take control of your life.

BRONWYN *becomes fervent, like a born-again preacher.*

You've gotta throw yourself into life. Be positive. Decide what your goals are and go for them! There must be things you want, Gillian.

GILLIAN: I don't know what I want…

BRONWYN: Adam! You want him—then go for it!

GILLIAN: C'mon, I haven't got a chance—

BRONWYN: Be positive, Gillo! Grab what you want from life. What have you got to lose? You're at rock bottom anyway.

GILLIAN: I s'pose.

BRONWYN: Put yourself in my hands!

GILLIAN: In your hands?

BRONWYN: Operation Adam!

GILLIAN: Oh-oh.

BRONWYN *stands* GILLIAN *up and starts doing her up… doing her hair, putting make-up on her. as she talks enthusiastically.* GILLIAN *is limp in her hands.*

BRONWYN: You can't sit around mooning after this guy. You haven't got anything to lose by going after him, have you? First thing we do is fix up how you look. You can do heaps with grooming and the right clothes. You have to *work* for beauty.

GILLIAN: Adam'd never look at me as—

BRONWYN: Wait till I've finished with you. He'll look at you in a whole new way. You said he's on the rocks with this Karen girl. This could be your big chance. I'll coach you. Teach you how to chat up guys.

GILLIAN: [*unconvinced*] Thanks, Bronwyn.

BRONWYN *starts holding clothes against* GILLIAN, *considering them.*

BRONWYN: If we get things that are cut the right way, we can hide your big bum. Mmm… we want a not-too-tarty dress with a slightly raunchy feel, without sacrificing elegance.

GILLIAN: Hunh?

BRONWYN: Put this on.

GILLIAN *changes into one of* BRONWYN'*s dresses.*

You can borrow it if you promise not to stretch it too much.

BIGGLES *booms out heartily as he comes into the house.*

BIGGLES: Bron! I've booked us in for hang-gliding.

BRONWYN *throws some shoes at* GILLIAN.

BRONWYN: We can try you out on John. So make a big entrance.

BRONWYN *rushes out to* BIGGLES *to stop him going in. She whispers to him, explaining. Meanwhile,* GILLIAN *puts on the high heels and speaks to the audience.*

GILLIAN: At this stage in stories like this, everything's meant to start getting better for The Ugly Duckling. That's me. I'm a beautiful swan now, right? Well, use your imaginations. The trouble is, I don't feel like a swan. I feel like Gillian with goo on her face.

BIGGLES: I'm coming in ready or not!

BIGGLES *barges in,* GILLIAN *poses awkwardly.*

Oh wow! You've done a fantastic job, Bron! You look great, Gillo. What's this guy's name?

BRONWYN: Adam.

GILLIAN: [*mortified*] You told him!?

BIGGLES: This Adam guy'll go for you, no worries.

BRONWYN: What we need is an *occasion* to show off the new Gillian.

BIGGLES: Don't they usually have end of year parties at your school?

BRONWYN: The perfect occasion!

GILLIAN: Oh, I wasn't planning on going…

BRONWYN: You have to go.

GILLIAN: But I hate parties.

BRONWYN: It's your big chance.

BIGGLES *slides up to* GILLIAN *lasciviously, putting an arm around her.*

BIGGLES: Go to the party and knock Adam's socks off. If he doesn't snap you up fast, he might get some competition from me.

GILLIAN: [*pushing his arm away*] Don't make fun of me, Biggles.

BIGGLES: I'm serious, mate. You look fabulous.

BRONWYN: I've put a lot of time and effort into the new you, Gillian. You can't just stay home with a paper bag on your head.

> GILLIAN *looks appealingly at* BIGGLES. *He nods encouragingly.* GILLIAN *smiles back gratefully.* BRONWYN *pushes* GILLIAN.

Off you go.

The school party. The room is dimly lit, rock music is playing in the background. Kids and dummies make up the group. One kid is rolling around on the floor with a dummy, 'pashing off'. KAREN *looks miserable, and is drinking heavily. Plastic cups and empty tinnies roll around the floor, where a few dummies have passed out.* GILLIAN *stands outside, watching this scene for a moment, before addressing the audience.*

GILLIAN: Remember the stuff I said about kids being vicious to each other? Well, parties are like a concentrated burst of all that viciousness. The rest of the week is like a rehearsal for Saturday night when the real manoeuvres go on.

> GILLIAN *uncomfortably enters the scene. She picks up a plastic cup and starts sipping on it nervously, constantly filling it up from a flagon. For a few moments, she stands awkwardly alone, drinking and tapping her foot joylessly to the music. Then she starts walking around craning her neck as if looking for someone she knows.*

This is the way I usually cope. I spend hours trying to look as if I'm looking for someone I know. It's better than standing around alone like a prawn.

> LYNETTE *totters over to her drunkenly.*

LYNETTE: Oh hi, Gillian. Looking for someone?

GILLIAN: Yeh, I am. But I don't think he's here.

LYNETTE: You look great, Gillian. Really different. You've done something different to your hair and you're wearing—

GILLIAN: [*supercool*] Oh, it's a bit different I guess.

LYNETTE: Anyway, you look great. Wouldn't recognise ya. [*She giggles drunkenly*] Shithouse party, eh. S'just all the dags from school.

GILLIAN: But it's meant to be a school party.

LYNETTE: Yeh, yeh, yeh. [*Giggling*] Don't listen to me—I'm pissed as a newt. [*She pokes at* GILLIAN] Hey, hey, have you seen Adam and Karen?

GILLIAN *looks round to see dagger looks exchanged across the room by* KAREN *and* ADAM.

LYNETTE: They're really on the rocks. Wanna bet?

GILLIAN: Oh well, I don't—

LYNETTE: For sure. It's been coming for ages. Karen hasn't got a chance of hanging on to him. She's stuffed.

LYNETTE *lurches over to* ADAM *and whispers something to him. He whispers something back and the two cackle and look at* KAREN. KAREN *bursts into tears and runs out of the room, clutching a wine cask.*

GILLIAN: I feel sick.

GILLIAN *climbs over the necking couple on the floor and goes outside.*

My other party survival tactic is to go and hide every now and then. The loo's no good cos some boofhead always lurches up and pounds on the door and forces me out. I'll escape to the garden for a bit. Aww, I know you're all thinking that tonight's my big chance with Adam. After a rest I'll come back and make an assault on him like Bronwyn would like. What've I got to lose?

Outside KAREN *is sitting on the ground, miserably nursing a wine cask. When* GILLIAN *sees her, she suddenly feels awkward and squeamish.*

Are you okay, Karen?

KAREN: Terrific.

GILLIAN: I'm sorry.

KAREN: Why should you be sorry?

GILLIAN: I'm sorry anyway.

KAREN: Is he still talking about me to everyone?

GILLIAN: Oh… not really. No.

KAREN: Did he tell you I'm dumb and never talk to him?

GILLIAN *nods.*

You know why? Whenever I said anything his face'd just go blank, his eyes'd go all glassy—I could tell he wasn't listening. I didn't want to bore him.

GILLIAN: Yeh, he's in love with the sound of his own voice.

KAREN: You betcha.

KAREN *and* GILLIAN *exchange a slight smile. There is an awkward silence.* GILLIAN *wants to push this brief moment of contact.*

GILLIAN: I understand how you must be—

KAREN: Ya reckon?

GILLIAN: Well, I mean, I know you must be feeling pretty… um…

KAREN *huddles away from* GILLIAN.

KAREN: You better leave me alone. I look ugly when I cry.

GILLIAN: You don't look ugly. And anyway, I don't care if—

KAREN: I do. Just leave me alone.

GILLIAN: Oh. Okay.

GILLIAN *sidles away.* GILLIAN *nervously ventures back into the party. She refills her glass and perches on a couch awkwardly. She tries not to notice when* ADAM *approaches her. He's cockily drunk.*

ADAM: Gillian.

GILLIAN: [*coolly*] Oh hi, Adam.

ADAM: I thought you didn't like parties.

GILLIAN: Oh well… you know…

ADAM: [*grinning*] Anyway, I'm glad you're here. You're looking really good. Different.

GILLIAN *smiles back flirtatiously.*

GILLIAN: Thanks.

ADAM: Did you hear I broke it off with Karen?

GILLIAN: Yeh, Lynette mentioned it was—
ADAM: About time too. Shit, what a dumbo that girl was. A spunk maybe, but nothing between the ears.

ADAM *snorts a contemptuous laugh.* GILLIAN *looks a little uneasy.*

GILLIAN: Adam, I don't think that's a fair thing to—
ADAM: Geez, I dunno how I lasted with her all that time. I mean, all she ever wanted to do was *maul* me. Enough to make ya sick.
GILLIAN: But you always said that you were the one who—
ADAM: [*laughing*] You know what she used to say sometimes? She—
GILLIAN: I don't want to hear. It's not fair to Karen.

GILLIAN *looks increasingly disgusted by him.* ADAM *talks pompously on, oblivious to her reactions.*

ADAM: You know what I mean, don't you. Like, a guy has to go around with his *equal*. His mental equal. Someone he can really talk to. Sure, looks are important. But anyone can look pretty okay. I mean, look how you've made yourself look better. [*He gives a charming grin*] This could be your big chance, Gillian.
GILLIAN: [*blurting out involuntarily*] I don't want you!

[*To audience*] What am I saying? My big chance and I'm throwing it away?

[*To* ADAM] I wouldn't want an up-himself, mindless conceited bore like you.

ADAM, *who is pretty drunk, is confused.*

ADAM: Hunh?

GILLIAN *turns triumphantly to the whole room.*

GILLIAN: I wouldn't touch a guy like him with a ten-foot pole.

With great dignity, GILLIAN *gets up, brushes herself off and strides off.* ADAM *ond* LYNETTE *watch her go, mouths hanging open.*

As soon as she leaves the party, GILLIAN *lets her exuberant reactions show. She bounds home, grinning broadly, hyped up; bubbling over.*

Did you see that? Amazing. God knows why I feel so bloody *happy* all of a sudden. I feel fan-bloody-tastic actually.

GILLIAN *squeezes herself in a hug and lets out a squeal of glee.*

Did you see the look on his face? Old Adam didn't know what hit him.

She's hopping around, full of nervous energy but not quite sure what to do with it. Words tumble out of her mouth in breathless excitement.

Wait till I tell Monica about what happened with Adam! She'll love it. Far out. Err… that reminds me. I've gotta go to school next week. And face them all. And Adam [*Giggling*] Oh. who cares? I pissed Adam off, didn't I? Right? So that's his problem. [*She hams up super-cool*] So I might as well play it pretty cool. Don't sweat it, Gillian. Play it cool. [*Babbling uncoolly again*] And anyway, anyway, no need to worry too much about school because it's exams soon and then I can get out of school, escape all those deadheads and take on the world. So I'd better Plan the Rest of My Life. That's a biggie. Have to think about that one for a while.

Anyway, it's gotta be better once you get out of school. I mean, you keep getting *older*, don't you? That's a fantastic thought really. Because eventually, you're not an adolescent anymore and then all this tortured adolescence stuff is over. I'll hardly notice I'm getting older till I suddenly discover I'm this incredibly dynamic woman. Right? Anyway, you'll have to excuse me—I've just got a million things to do.

GILLIAN *is grinning irrepressibly. She flings herself into a dramatic pose and squeals with delight.*

Gillian… you *animal!*

THE END

www.currency.com.au

Visit Currency Press' website now to:

- Buy your books online
- Browse through our full list of titles, from plays to screenplays, books on theatre, film and music, and more
- Choose a play for your school or amateur performance group by cast size and gender
- Obtain information about performance rights
- Find out about theatre productions and other performing arts news across Australia
- For students, read our study guides
- For teachers, access syllabus and other relevant information
- Sign up for our email newsletter

The performing arts publisher